Original title:
Under the Tropical Stars

Copyright © 2025 Creative Arts Management OÜ
All rights reserved.

Author: Sophia Kingsley
ISBN HARDBACK: 978-1-80581-702-4
ISBN PAPERBACK: 978-1-80581-229-6
ISBN EBOOK: 978-1-80581-702-4

Celestial Blossoms in the Breeze

The flowers giggle, swaying wide,
As fireflies dance, the insects glide.
A monkey swings, a prankster bold,
Stealing snacks from friends, oh so bold.

Laughter erupts as coconuts fall,
They hit the ground with a comical brawl.
A parrot squawks, its voice so bright,
Every night feels like a silly flight.

Dreaming Beneath an Ocean of Stars

Bubbles pop as fish wear hats,
Jellyfish jiggle, prancing like spats.
A sea turtle floats, so carefree,
Plotting his heist for the next cup of tea.

Stars twinkle brightly, like winking eyes,
As crabs tap dance, oh what a surprise!
Sandy toes and giggles abound,
Under the sky, joy is profound.

Shadows of the Palms at Midnight

Palm trees whisper, sharing their glee,
While a cat thinks it's a couch, oh what a spree!
A lizard slips past with a wink and a smirk,
As night creeps in to play and lurk.

The moon chuckles, a bright silver dime,
Counting the crickets, keeping the time.
With shadows that dance and giggles that flow,
The night is a party, come join the show!

A Serenade of Tropical Nights

The breeze croons softly, a playful tune,
As frogs take the stage, one is a buffoon.
A tree frog leaps, wearing a crown,
Singing for all, he won't back down.

The stars wink back, like tiny spotlights,
While fireflies join, twinkling with delights.
An otter slides in, with a splash and a cheer,
Creating a ruckus, bringing good cheer.

The Cosmic Symphony of Dusk

As twilight hums a cheery tune,
The crickets join, a silly croon.
Frogs in tuxedos leap with grace,
While fireflies flash, a glowing chase.

Jupiter winks, the planets chuckle,
A squirrel's dance turns into a shuffle.
Stars giggle, twinkle like a mirthful jest,
In this cosmic circus, we're all a guest.

Melodies of the Night Bloom

At night, the blooms begin to sway,
Whispering secrets, come what may.
A daisy in bloom starts to jive,
While sleepy tulips laugh and thrive.

The moon sings sweet, a silly song,
With shadows prancing, all night long.
Petals flutter, like they can't decide,
Whether to dance or take a ride.

Shadows Dancing with the Moon

Shadows pirouette, all in a route,
A sneaky cat joins in, no doubt.
The moon is a spotlight, beams on the ground,
As giggles of owls echo around.

Breezes chuckle and rustle the trees,
Pointing fingers at the buzzing bees.
A mystical night, with laughter galore,
Every little creature wanting more.

Chasing the Silvery Horizon

Horizons stretch with a playful tease,
As raccoons swagger, prancing with ease.
Stars wink as if sharing a joke,
While palm fronds sway, giggling they poke.

Beneath the sky, the world comes alive,
A merry band of critters, they thrive.
Chasing dreams like butterflies roam,
In this wacky night, all creatures feel home.

Fireflies and Faint Echoes

Fireflies dance with no real plan,
They bump and wiggle, oh what a clan!
Each little flicker, a bright little tease,
Lighting the night like a million bees.

A croaking frog joins the leafy choir,
Singing off-key, but he's filled with desire.
A firefly lands on my funny nose,
Just a brief moment, then off it goes!

Journey of the Heart Beneath Starlight

On a night-trip, the heart takes flight,
With twinkly friends, oh what a sight!
Did Cupid miss with his awkward aim?
Fell for a girl who forgot my name!

We counted stars, but some just fell,
Like my attempts at a sweet love spell.
Her laughter echoed, a bright shiny ring,
Got tangled in thoughts - and a mosquito sting!

Celestial Canopy Over Enchanted Waters

Reflections dance on the shimmering lake,
A fish jumps high, causing a shake!
It seems a mermaid, all shiny and bold,
But it's just my buddy, trying to be gold!

With splashes and laughter, we kayak in cheer,
Who knew this water would bring such fear?
An otter pops up, gives a cheeky grin,
And we're left wondering where to begin!

The Call of Sirens in the Night

Heard a melody floating on air,
Thought it was sirens, led to despair.
But turns out it's just Steve with his ukulele,
Singing off-key, calling us to rally!

We danced in circles, our moves were wild,
The night became madness, we felt like kids.
With laughter and snacks beneath the moon,
Who knew late nights turned chaos to croon?

Echoes of the Tropical Nightingale

A bird sang loud, drank coconut cold,
His dance was silly, so bold, so bold.
With a parrot as backup, they worked it out,
The jungle's a stage, that's without doubt.

Bamboo snaps, as if on cue,
A monkey claps, he's in full view.
They laughed at shadows by the moon's light,
While lizards tap-danced, what a sight!

A Carousel of Celestial Wonders

The stars spun 'round like a merry-go,
Clowns on surfboards, oh what a show!
A turtle juggles with shells on his knees,
While dolphins giggle and dance with ease.

Moonbeams twirl, they play tag with the breeze,
While crabs do the cha-cha, with style that'll please.
Each wave that crashes, a comedic splash,
As fish start laughing, making quite the bash!

Star-trails Over Ocean Waves

A fish in a tux, with a top hat so grand,
Caught a wave, surfed right to the land.
He winked at the sky, said 'Watch me dive!'
While the sea turtles chimed, 'We're lucky to thrive.'

With trails made of stardust, they raced the night,
Sardines on skateboards joined in the flight.
Lobsters played drums, a rhythmic delight,
While seagulls squawked, dancing left and right!

The Ethereal Glow of Island Nights

Glowing lanterns flicker, like fireflies dance,
A chicken in shades took a flashy stance.
The coconut cocktails spilled with a cheer,
As the crickets hummed, no need for fear.

A hula girl twirled, lost her own shoe,
An octopus waltzed, pulling kids too.
Under palm trees, they spun around,
What a night—laughter is the best sound!

Stories beneath the Indigo Sky

Beneath the twilight's splash, they prance,
A raccoon wearing shades, doing a dance.
Sneaky monkeys play poker with cards,
While flamingos judge from their fancy yards.

The toucan tells jokes, each punchline a hit,
As crickets laugh loudly, they just can't quit.
A parrot sips soda, hiccups in glee,
Says, 'I lost my beak in the last jamboree!'

Beacons of the Lost Tropics

Luminous lizards glow like neon signs,
While frogs croon love songs in rhythmic lines.
A turtle's slow-motion race steals the show,
Cheering crowds of fireflies make quite a glow.

Cockatoos serve drinks from a coconut tree,
With umbrellas and laughter, oh what glee!
They toast to the night with a bright, silly grin,
In this raucous gala where chaos begins!

Secrets of the Nocturnal Realm

A walrus in glasses peruses a book,
On how to make friends with a curious crook.
The sloth takes a selfie, but what a delay,
As he snoozes through moments, the night slips away.

The owls hold a conference, debating their names,
Should they stick with 'Hooters' or start all new games?
While bats play charades, flapping around,
The punchline erupts, and the laughter resounds!

The Calm Aglow with Night's Promise

In the calm of the dusk, all critters convene,
A crab playing chess, what a sight to be seen!
A dolphin flips pancakes, while giggling with pride,
As the moon winks at everyone feasting outside.

Grasshoppers hop in sync, a dance on the ground,
Unplanned and delightful, their joy is profound.
Fireworks from otters, a splish and a splash,
While friendships bloom bright in this whimsical bash!

Celestial Serenades of the Night

The crickets play their funny tune,
As fireflies dance beneath the moon.
A parrot squawks a joke so loud,
Even the dolphins laugh, they're proud.

The stars above seem to twinkle back,
At the beach party, what a knack!
A coconut falls, rollin' astray,
Who knew pineapples liked to play?

A conch shell sings a silly song,
As surfers try to dance along.
The tide comes in, a wave of cheer,
Now's the time to grab a beer!

With laughter woven in the breeze,
We'll share these moments, if you please.
The night won't end with just a few,
Stay close, my friend, we'll dance 'til two!

Lanterns of the Warm Breeze

The lanterns sway like drunk old pals,
As we tell tales of our grand fails.
A crab in a bowtie spins around,
With every step, he shall be crowned!

The laughter lifts upon the air,
As shorts are stained with dripping fare.
Is that a fish? No, just a shoe!
The ocean's playing tricks on you!

With drinks in hand, we toast a toast,
To the giant wave that we liked most.
But who fell flat—was it you or me?
The night's a blur, let's wait and see!

So let's not trip on what's ahead,
We'll dance until we lose our head.
Underneath the vibrant flames,
We'll make up rhymes and funny names!

Whispers Between the Palms

The palms are chuckling, swaying low,
Sharing secrets that we don't know.
A lizard giggles as it struts,
While all our snacks fall to the cuts.

A pineapple wears a tiny hat,
Declaring, "Don't you dare touch that!"
As we tease the waves with our bare feet,
The tide comes in, oh what a feat!

Now a small crab has joined the fray,
Dancing with us all night and day.
He tells bad jokes, we all laugh loud,
A comedian beneath the crowd.

In shadows deep, we share our quirks,
With the moonlight guiding all our works.
So gather round, let's vent our dreams,
In this laughter, life's better, it seems!

Moonlit Dances on Sandy Shores

The moon is full, my friend, oh dear,
Just watch the way it winks and leers.
A crab's got moves, it's quite a sight,
Who knew the critters could dance right?

We stumble on the sandy ground,
Tripping over shells we've found.
With each grand twirl, we burst with glee,
As laughter echoes, wild and free.

The waves applaud our goofy show,
As seagulls watch, they're in the know.
A flip-flop flies, a true disaster,
But we keep dancing, ever faster!

So lift your drinks, toast to the sand,
A comedic night, so unplanned.
We'll laugh and twirl until we drop,
In moonlit bliss, we'll never stop!

A Symphony of Crickets and Waves

Crickets chirp a merry tune,
While waves dance beneath the moon.
A coconut falls with a thud,
And fish giggle in the mud.

The parrot squawks a wise old sage,
He'll tell you jokes from the jungle page.
A crab moonwalks, what a sight!
As seashells hum of pure delight.

Laughter echoes off the sea,
As palm trees sway, wild and free.
The starfish tosses in the sand,
Dreaming of being in a band!

Beneath the bright celestial crowd,
The beach throws a party, loud and proud.
With every wave that splashes by,
The ocean waves a wink and sigh.

Nightfall's Palette Over Paradise

Colors blend in hues so bright,
The sky paints smiles, a true delight.
A mojito slips from tumbler's grace,
As limes giggle with a citrus face.

Chickens strut, they own the place,
In feathered coats, they run the race.
A sunburned tourist, lost and dazed,
Fumbles their camera, slightly phased.

The stars above play hide and seek,
While a mango munches, sweet and sleek.
With every toast, the laughter swells,
Under the breeze, where joy dwells.

A drumming beat from a distant shore,
Invites the brave to dance and roar.
With flip-flops flying, spirits rise,
While the moon winks down with surprise.

Starlit Dreams on the Island's Edge

A hammock sways in the night's embrace,
As sleepy crabs hold a gentle race.
Fireflies flicker, a light ballet,
While palm trees sway, come out to play.

A fish leaps up, a flying star,
Spilling secrets from afar.
A turtle snoozes, dreaming wide,
Of treasure buried deep inside.

The ocean hums a lullaby sweet,
While a sea cucumber claims its seat.
The silhouette of a distant boat,
Goes fishing for dreams, that's all she wrote!

Stars twinkle like confetti tossed,
Celebrating the laughter not lost.
With every splash, every little cheer,
The magic sprawls, so crystal clear.

The Secrets the Ocean Carries

The ocean whispers tales untold,
Of mermaids' giggles and treasure bold.
A starfish laughs at the fish who splash,
While conch shells plan a secret bash.

A dolphin plays with a beach ball bright,
While sea urchins hide, frights from the night.
With a flick of a fin, the moonlight glows,
Rolling in waves, the sun always knows.

Coconuts toasting, they clink with zest,
As jellyfish groove in their jelly best.
An octopus tries a stand-up act,
With all eight limbs, what a whacky fact!

The ocean carries both joy and jest,
Each bubble bursting with a cheeky jest.
In the nighttime breeze, let's raise a cheer,
For the laughs and the secrets that we hold dear.

Secrets Woven in the Night Air

In the hammock I lie, dreaming sweet,
A coconut falls, it's my head's new seat.
The crickets chirp their comical tunes,
While a raccoon steals cookies beneath the moons.

Fireflies flicker, they dance with glee,
One landed on my nose, how rude can it be?
With laughter spilling, I spill my drink,
The night is silly, what more can I think?

The Lure of the Evening Tide

The waves whisper secrets, they giggle and tease,
Shells acting like lawyers, with sand as their fees.
I build a grand castle, it crumbles with flair,
It's a sandy disaster; my throne's a beach chair.

Seagulls squawk loudly, they're jesting my meal,
As they swoop down swiftly to steal my great deal.
With a splash and a laugh, I give them a shove,
This beach trip is chaos, but oh, how I love!

Gazing at the Cosmic Canvas

Stars strut and wink, in their shiny attire,
One tumbled down, claiming 'I want to retire!'
With comets that giggle and planets that spin,
I wonder if aliens just want to join in.

A shooting star zips by, yelling 'Catch me quick!'
I reach for the sky, but I'm not too slick.
My toes in the sand, I dance like a fool,
The cosmos is laughing; I'm breaking the rule!

Echoes in the Ferns' Embrace

The ferns wave hello, with their leafy ballet,
While a chameleon chats about colors in play.
A frog leaps nearby, doing high-flying tricks,
As night unfolds tales with her quirky little picks.

The whispers of foliage tell jokes in the breeze,
'Why did the plant hide? For fear of disease!'
With giggles from bugs, the night comes alive,
In the forest's embrace, we hilariously thrive.

Beneath Cascades of Light

In a hammock swaying high,
A mosquito buzzed a lullaby.
I swatted left, then right, oh dear,
My dance moves caused a ruckus here.

Coconut drinks with little straws,
Sip too fast, you'll find the flaws.
With every gulp, the world spins round,
Falling out makes quite the sound!

The palm fronds whisper jokes at night,
As crickets chirp with sheer delight.
Who knew the breeze could tease so well?
I'm laughing hard; it's hard to tell!

Frogs in chorus, what a show!
They croak as if they're in the know.
Beneath the glow and mischief's sigh,
We raise our cups and laugh, oh my!

The Night's Embrace on Silken Waters

The moonlit ripples laugh and play,
Fish jump high, then drift away.
I tossed a line, with hopes of gold,
But all I caught was stories told.

A boat ride was our grand design,
Yet here I am, tangled in twine!
The oars went left, and I went right,
Caught in a splash, what a sight!

We chased the waves as laughter chased,
Each splash a joke, a silly taste.
A starrry night, a joint delight,
Soaking wet, we all took flight.

With every splash, we'd scream and yell,
"Did you see that?!" "Oh, do tell!"
The night was ours, and time stood still,
The giggles echoed, pure thrill!

Lanterns in the Jungle

Lights dangle like forgotten dreams,
Swinging low with silly schemes.
A monkey stole my snack last night,
Now he's the king, and I'm his plight!

With each lantern, a bug's delight,
I swat one down, it takes a flight.
Buzzing 'round like they own the place,
Their tiny dance puts me to chase!

Laughter rings through leafy ferns,
As creatures plot their fun-filled turns.
"Step right up!" the chubby frog croaks,
His talent show makes us all chokes!

On paths lit bright with giggles shared,
Who knew nature could be so paired?
With critters acting, nature's jest,
In this green maze, we find our best!

A Tapestry of Stars and Shadows

Look up high, the stars do twirl,
Each one a wink, each one a swirl.
Are they laughing at our mere plight?
Got lost again, but what a night!

The shadows dance, they take a bow,
"Come join us, human," says the cow.
But mistaking it for moonlit art,
I tripped and tumbled, that's just smart!

As fireflies blink their playful tunes,
I tried to catch one in the dunes.
But it zoomed off with quite the flair,
I'm left below with messy hair!

With giggles echoing soft and bright,
We bask in joy beneath the night.
This tapestry we weave with glee,
Is an endless dance of silly spree!

Veils of Celestial Mists

In the garden of dreams where the fireflies dance,
A chicken clucks loudly, insisting on chance.
The moon wears a grin, a cheeky delight,
While critters conspire to party all night.

A squirrel named Freddy juggles ripe fruits,
With laughter erupting from all the weird roots.
A mongoose in shades plays the bongo with flair,
As vines twist and sway, shaking off every care.

The stars throw confetti, it covers the ground,
While crickets debate who makes the best sound.
There's a llama in sandals, it prances with glee,
In this whimsical moment, we're all wild and free.

So come join the revelry, let worries depart,
Embrace the absurd, let it dance in your heart.
For laughter's the compass, and joy is our quest,
In this night of delight, we are truly blessed.

A Woven Tale of Night's Whispers

As shadows stretch long, the jungle awakes,
A parrot tells jokes while the lantern bug brakes.
A sloth in a hammock, too lazy to swing,
Announces it's time for the night's silly fling.

The owls hoot in chorus, creating a band,
With beats from a beetle, who's bruting its hand.
The cheese from the mouse brought great cheer to the crowd,
While a frog starts to croak, sounding quite proud.

The stars peek with mischief, sly glimmers of light,
While laughter erupts in the warmth of the night.
A raccoon in slippers flips pancakes with flair,
As jellybeans rain down, a sweet, sticky air.

So gather your friends, let laughter ignite,
And dance with the critters until morning light.
These woven tales echo, delightful and bright,
In a world full of whimsy, everything feels right.

Shadows of Coconut Trees

Coconuts dance in the breeze,
While I dodge falling fruit with ease.
The palm trees whisper secrets near,
As crabs plot with a hint of cheer.

A lizard sings a silly song,
Claiming he's the king, yet wrong.
The night is bright, the moon's a clown,
Making waves splash all around.

An owl hoots at the moonlit jest,
Wondering why I never rest.
I sip my drink, in laughter's grip,
As stars above begin to flip.

With every splash, an echo lives,
As coconut jokes the ocean gives.
Tomorrow's harvest tastes so sweet,
But first, I'll dance with shuffling feet.

Silhouettes Against a Distant Horizon

The horizon shows a dancing line,
While my shadow thinks it's divine.
With every leap and every bound,
I'm a circus act, upside down!

A palm leaf tickles the sky,
As I try to reach it up high.
The sun rolls in, the moon rolls out,
My shadow's giggling without doubt.

Fish jump up to take a look,
As I pretend to write a book.
It's mainly recipes for fun,
Like how to dance and how to run!

A breeze comes in, whispering jokes,
As laughter echoes with the folks.
The stars will join our nightly plays,
With silly pranks and bright displays.

The Night Sky's Tropical Tapestry

The sky's a quilt, starry and bright,
While I sip fruit punch, feeling light.
With patterns made of laughter's thread,
I dream of coconuts near my head.

Who knew that stars could be such clowns?
Shuffling about in cosmic gowns.
They wink and jiggle, playfully bold,
As I recount tales I've been told.

The moon grins wide, revealing a joke,
About a fish that tried to poke.
Sprinkling giggles on seashells and sand,
I can't help but clap my hands.

So here I lay, with stars overhead,
Listening to dreams that dance in my head.
Oh, what a night, and who would believe,
That laughter is all we really need!

Glimmers of Light on Still Waters

Reflections ripple with a wink,
As I sit back and start to think.
A fish jumps up with a cheeky grin,
Splashing my drink with a daring spin!

The water shimmers, playing tricks,
As I recount my life's odd picks.
A crab crabs up to join the fun,
Saying, 'This party's just begun!'

The stars above throw a dazzling show,
As I try to catch the light, oh no!
But every splash and every laugh,
Keeps me giggling, like a silly calf.

So let's toast to waves and shimmering sights,
To nighttime stories and endless delights.
With every giggle, my worries fade,
As light on the water swiftly wades.

Footprints in the Moonlit Sand

I danced with crabs, they clapped their claws,
My feet were lost, and so were my flaws.
I slipped on seaweed, oh what a sight,
The ocean laughed back, it was pure delight.

A beach ball bounced off my silly hat,
Even the dolphins chuckled at that.
With laughter echoing through the night air,
I waved to the seagulls, not a single care.

Sandy footprints leading to nowhere,
A treasure map drawn, or was it a dare?
I followed my giggles, oh what a tease,
Only to find my flip-flops at ease.

So here I lie, a star in my eye,
The tide rolls in, and I know not why.
But who needs answers when there's such fun,
I'll count the starfish, and call it a run.

A Tidesong of Memories

The waves would hum as I lost my hat,
Float like a whale? No, more like a cat.
A surfboard sandwich, I took a big bite,
Mmmm, salty, crunchy—what a delight!

Seagulls swooped down for a quick little snack,
Who knew my fries would get such a hack?
I waved them goodbye, they honked back in glee,
I'll save you a crumb, if you find me a sea!

A jellyfish jiggle, a crab in a snatch,
He pinched my toe—oh what a catch!
I laughed as he stomped on the soft, wet earth,
Claiming this shoreline, oh what is this worth?

A memory made, with laughter at play,
Tidal tales carry the night away.
So here's to the moments, both silly and grand,
Let's dance to the rhythm, arm in arm, hand in hand.

The Serengeti of Stars Beyond the Sea

The stars winked down like playful friends,
Each twinkle a nod as the night never ends.
I lay on the beach, counting spots on my nose,
While conch shells conspired in whispers and prose.

A crab in a tuxedo tangoed along,
With seahorses clapping to the coconut song.
They welcomed the sunset, donning their best,
While moonbeams pirouetted, they truly impressed.

I laughed at a fish who borrowed my shades,
"Keep them," I said, "and enjoy your charades!"
He splashed in the surf, making quite the scene,
While I snickered at clouds, all fluffy and clean.

The constellations giggled, a sparkling crew,
Holding hands with the mist, painting dreams anew.
So let's toast to the waves and the silly parade,
Life's a funny dance, with laughter displayed!

Strumming the Harp of Night

The moon plucked strings, in a soft, sweet tune,
While I danced with shadows, under a balloon.
A octopus fiddled on a golden harp,
Making melodies that made my heart warp.

A parrot squawked from an old palm tree,
"Join my band, come sing with me!"
I tried a high note, but ended with squawks,
The sand shook its head, just like the rocks.

Then dolphins jumped in, tail-twirling around,
As I strummed my ukulele, a harmonic sound.
We played till the sunrise, a concert so grand,
A night filled with laughter, oh, wasn't it planned?

So here in the twilight, as fun takes its flight,
I swing with the crickets, in the soft, warm night.
Let the music keep playing, a tune full of cheer,
For every silly moment, let's hold it most dear!

Luminous Dreams of the Tropics

A parrot tried to sing a tune,
While he danced around a coconut moon.
But in his rhythm, he lost his way,
And tripped on a crab, oh what a play!

The fireflies giggle, they light up the scene,
As the iguana grins, he's truly a queen.
With sand underfoot, we laugh in a line,
Searching for shoes, well isn't it fine?

A mango fell ripe, it splattered my head,
I tried catching dreams; instead, I caught dread.
"Next time" I sighed, "I won't dream too loud,"
While poking the seaweed, oh so proud!

Off in the distance, the conch shells would blow,
But the crabs stole my snacks, saying, "No, no, no!"
So we danced on the shore, our laughter like waves,
Under the glow, we were all just a bunch of knaves!

Phosphorescent Tides at Dusk

The waves were transparent, like jellyfish art,
I paddled my feet when I fell with a start.
Hiccupping fish vowed to jump in my lap,
While the starry night giggled, "You're quite the chap!"

A toucan with sunglasses strutted on by,
He winked at the moon with a mischievous sigh.
"Join me!" he shouted, "Let's party till dawn!"
But I lost my drink to a cheeky chameleon.

The sand made me sticky, my toes felt like glue,
But sandcastle dreams were all I could do.
I built a great fortress, but a wave had a fit,
And washed all my towers, oh what a split!

A crab served me nachos, it couldn't be real,
With salsa so spicy, I squealed like a wheel.
"Next round's on the waves!" I teased with a grin,
While the stars held their breath—let the fun begin!

Celestial Reflections on Water

Beneath the gnarled palm, I took my sweet chair,
My drink made of coconut, with a flair.
The waves played like dancers, all splashy and bright,
Tickling my toes in the warm breezy night.

A floating banana split joined in my game,
"Hey buddy!" I chuckled, "You're truly a name!"
But a dog with a snorkel swam past with a splash,
Saying, "Chill out, dude! You're way too brash!"

A fish in a tutu performed on my plate,
Then slipped off in shock, as I asked for more fate.
The night whispered secrets while stars began to twink,
I thought I saw twins of a ghostly pink wink!

So we laughed and we played, till our giggles found home,
Chasing reflections that stuffed us with foam.
We raised our drinks high, as the sea echoed loud,
In a night full of whimsy, we danced like a crowd!

The Soul of an Enchanted Evening

A boa constrictor showed me his hat,
And told me the secrets of where to find that.
But the turtles just laughed, while the frogs played the drums,
As I fumbled my drink with some wild, wiggly chums.

The moon played cards with the sun of the morn,
And it reignited tales that were slightly worn.
A swaying palm tree whispered tales of great woe,
As I lost my marbles, no one would know!

Then suddenly there came a surprise party bug,
Who offered me salsa, and a generous shrug.
My heart raced with laughter as I joined in the fun,
Chasing flashlights that flickered, we'd all just begun!

So here's to the night, where we dance and we cheer,
Sipping sweet cocktails, shouting "We're here!"
With every twinkle and gust in the air,
We found in the mirth, a world beyond compare!

Lullabies of the Jungle Sky

In the jungle's cozy croon,
Monkeys swing with silver spoons.
Bananas drop from leafy hands,
As laughter echoes through the lands.

A parrot sings a silly song,
While the sloths just hum along.
Crocodiles in laughter glide,
Chasing dreams on moonlit tide.

The frogs play tag on lily pads,
While tigers nudge at sleepy lads.
A breeze that tickles every nose,
Whispers tales of nightly prose.

And as the night draws ever near,
The sounds of joy are all we hear.
Crickets join the chorus free,
In this jungle jubilee.

The Dance of Fireflies at Dusk

In the dusk, a twinkle spree,
Fireflies dance in jubilee.
They flit in patterns, round and round,
Like little lights that pulse and bound.

A gecko's laugh, a playful shout,
"Hey, catch me if you can!" it touts.
But fireflies shine with all their might,
They wiggle away in pure delight.

A chicken joins the flickering crew,
With feathers bright, it struts anew.
It tries to boogie, oh what a sight,
But ends up kicking dirt in flight.

Once the sun retreats with style,
These glowing gems bring forth a smile.
In this ballet of buzzing cheer,
The night transforms, it's crystal clear.

Embracing the Velvet Night

The night unfurls a velvet sheet,
Where bugs and critters mix and meet.
A snake with glitter in its scales,
Goes searching for sweet, fruity trails.

A rabbit hops, in shades of gray,
Joking with stars that twinkle play.
It sneaks a taste of moonlit pie,
With giggles shared among the sky.

The owls are hooting snappy tunes,
With catchy lines to lighten moons.
A skunk at dusk rolls on the floor,
Saying, "We need to party more!"

As night falls down like a big hug,
Join the chorus, don't be a bug.
Under velvet skies we shine bright,
In perfect harmony tonight.

Silhouettes Against a Starry Veil

Silhouettes twirl in lazy flight,
Swaying gently in the night.
A llama prances, full of flair,
Wearing shades like it's summer air.

A turtle slides with chill finesse,
While crickets hum, they do confess.
"Oh, what fun!" they chirp with glee,
"When dancing here, we're truly free!"

With every leap, the shadows sway,
Stealing glances, come what may.
It's a cha-cha with the moon,
As palm trees sway, singing a tune.

And in the midst of all this cheer,
A skunk winks; it's crystal clear.
In joyous steps, we make our trails,
In playful arcs, as laughter sails.

A Nightbird's Ode to the Cosmos

In twilight's glow, a bird took flight,
Singing to stars, what a funny sight!
He chirped of planets, and worms galore,
"Just a little longer, I'll find more!"

His friends all chuckled, dismissing the fuss,
"Those stars, dear mate, are too far for us!
But if you see a shiny, tasty treat,
Then let's have a picnic, oh, what a feat!"

They danced and twirled, in moonbeam's cheer,
Daytime worries? Not a thought here!
The Milky Way served as their heavenly path,
As crickets joined in with their light-hearted laugh.

So if you hear laughter in the night,
It's just the birds, feeling light and bright!
While planets may spin, and comets may zoom,
We're all just here, sharing joy in the gloom.

Songs of the Evening Breeze.

The breeze came dancing, all merry and spry,
Tickling the branches, oh my, oh my!
It whispered sweet nothings to all that it found,
Even the crabs, who scuttled around.

A coconut fell with a loud, funny thud,
The palm trees giggled, "What a clumsy dud!"
Seashells laughed, as they clinked in delight,
"Let's sing to the moon, it's a magical night!"

The frogs joined in, with a ribbit and croak,
Creating a symphony, laughter's sweet cloak.
From sand to the sea, oh sweet lullabies,
A humor fest brews beneath the starry skies.

So when evening comes and the world starts to sway,
Join in the fun, let your troubles drift away!
Let the breeze serenade you with tales from afar,
And dance with the shadows, as bright as a star!

Whispers of the Moonlit Canopy

Up in the branches, the critters convene,
Beneath a bright moon, such a silly scene.
A raccoon in spectacles, reading a book,
"Did you hear about planets? Oh, take a look!"

The possums exclaimed, with wide, twinkling eyes,
"We've heard of a place where the cheese fills the skies!"

"Let's pack up our dreams and unite in this quest,
To find all the snacks the galaxy blessed!"

With giggles of joy, they set off with cheer,
Past glow-in-the-dark mushrooms but never a fear.
Each step was a chuckle, every branch a jest,
As they chased vivid tales, not one would rest.

So when the night whispers, and laughter's the tune,
Join the secret meetings, under the moon.
In the forest of dreams, where humor grows free,
We're all cosmic critters, as wild as can be!

Nightfall Over Paradise

As daylight fades, and shadows embrace,
The island ignites, a whimsical place.
Laughter erupts from the waves on the sand,
With crabs in their tuxes, looking quite grand!

A parrot in sequins, takes center stage,
"Here's a joke, folks, let me turn the page!
Why did the fish swim against the tide?
To get to the party with style and pride!"

The fireflies twinkled, in sync with the beat,
While turtles performed an impressive retreat.
"Dance with us all," sang the night breeze,
"Let's celebrate life with a splash and a tease!"

So when night falls soft, on this paradise shore,
Know that joy is the language, forever more.
With rhythm of laughter, and friendships so bright,
We'll frolic together, 'neath the moonlight!

In the Embrace of Foliage and Stars

With coconuts cradled in a hammock sway,
The fireflies dance like they're on display.
A parrot squawks out a punny cheer,
While frogs serenade us with their weird leer.

The moon's a spotlight for the party crowd,
As we toast our drinks, feeling oh so proud.
Lizards strut like they own the scene,
Who knew reptiles could be so keen?

A toucan joins, with a beak so bright,
Chiming in with jokes, all through the night.
Beneath palm trees, we laugh with glee,
As nature's comedy unfolds for free.

So let's sway with the wind and hug a tree,
In this night of whimsy, just you and me.
For in the tropics, the stars shine high,
And even the crickets are here to try.

Lyrics Written in the Nightmist

Lurking in shadows, the critters all scheme,
While the moonlight's a glow on my ice cream dream.
A tiger-striped cat tiptoes with flair,
Looking for mischief prowling somewhere.

A kookaburra laughs at my silly dance,
He flaps his wings for a laugh-chance.
With each strum of the guitar, faux pas abound,
Even the mangoes start falling down.

Stars throw confetti, they twinkle and tease,
While my friend spills soda—oh what a breeze!
We wiggle on grass, like it's a big game,
Nature's our stage, igniting the flame.

From firefly fireworks to the crickets' chic beat,
Every glance, every giggle, makes the night so sweet.
So join in the revelry, let's not pretend,
For the laughter and chaos will never end!

The Allure of the Cosmic Night

The stars take a bow, as the night hits its peak,
A monkey swings in, with an ear-piercing shriek.
He juggles ripe bananas, what a clown,
While I try to keep my snacks safe and sound.

The clouds drift by with a giggly hue,
As a raccoon pops up in a tutu, too!
With lost socks as confetti, he starts to prance,
Suddenly, even the trees join the dance.

An owl hoots a melody, wise yet absurd,
He gives us advice, though it's quite blurred.
The night whispers secrets of giggles and more,
As we flip-flop around on the sandy shore.

So grab your friends and sway to the beat,
While the breeze adds rhythm to our laughter's heat.
In this cosmic whirl of fun and delight,
We'll paint the night silly—what a sight!

Nightfall's Radiance in the Tropics

As night falls gently, it's quite a show,
The tropics pull smiles, like a warm glow.
A crab's got moves, doing the conga line,
While I trip on grass—oh, moonshine divine!

The stars peek down, with a twinkly grin,
A chorus of critters joins in the din.
A dancing iguana, bright as a flame,
Turns the night into a whimsical game.

Palm trees wave like they know how to groove,
While our laughter echoes, setting the mood.
From bongo beats to a comical chat,
We're spiced up with joy, can you handle that?

So, come take a dip in this wild, fun sea,
With vibrations of laughter, we're wild and free.
Under these skies where dreams take flight,
We'll cherish the wackiness of the night!

The Pulse of Nature's Nightfall

Beetles dance with silly flair,
As frogs croak tunes, a crazy choir.
The moon winks down, a friendly glare,
While owls hoot jokes that never tire.

Lizards dive, so spry and quick,
Chasing shadows, they slip and slide.
The breeze plays tricks, a playful trick,
As fireflies light the evening tide.

Crickets chirp the silliest song,
A rhythm that will make you grin.
The night is lively; it won't be long,
'Til giggles turn to a dance within.

With each rustle, laughter swells,
Nature's jesters take the stand.
In this parade, the night compels,
The fun is vast across the land.

Harmonies of the Evening Breeze

The wind whispers secrets, oh so sly,
Tickling leaves as they sway and spin.
A playful parrot learns to fly,
While night critters tease with a grin.

Dancing palm fronds sway to the beat,
As a sloth snores loud, missing the cue.
The stars laugh softly, oh so sweet,
While a catfish wears its best shoe.

Mice gather round for a midnight snack,
Look out! A sudden leap and flop!
Nature's kitchen is quite the act,
A crab rolls in, yelling, "Stop!"

Amidst the ruckus, joy does swell,
As shadows join in this light-hearted cheer.
The evening breeze knows all too well,
That laughter's the language we hold dear.

Nightscapes Beneath Archer's Fire

Stars twinkle like eyes dancing bright,
As critters prance in whimsical glee.
A rabbit hops, what a funny sight,
While the moon chuckles, mischievously free.

The crabs are having a clumsy race,
With jerky moves, they scuttle and shake.
Each twirl they make, a comical face,
As they dream of a sumptuous cake.

Bats swoop low, chasing their tails,
Drifting through cotton-candy clouds.
While frogs tap dance in funny scales,
The night wears laughter like a shroud.

With every sound, giggles bloom,
As shadows play, carefree and spry.
Night reveals fun in every room,
With nature's pulse, both loud and sly.

In the Stillness of Midnight Isles

In quiet nooks, where critters dwell,
A hermit crab struts, oh so brash.
The fish exchange tales, giggling well,
As the waves toss in a nightly splash.

Parrots sing ballads in tuneful glee,
A chorus so vibrant, wild and loud.
While stingrays glide, carefree and free,
Making ripples in a giggling crowd.

Laughter echoes in coral caves,
As dolphins leap, performing tricks.
The calm night air, it surely saves,
The whimsy found in nature's flicks.

So join the dance of the midnight show,
With every shift, the smiles abound.
In this stillness, laughter will grow,
As joy reveals magic all around.

The Starlit Serenade of Wanderers

Beneath the twinkling laughter on high,
The wanderers dance as crickets sigh.
They trip on roots and swap tall tales,
As fireflies join, like tiny gales.

One claims he sold his shoes to a ghost,
While another insists he once caught a toast.
They giggle and snort, with stars in their eyes,
What's fact and what's fiction, oh what a surprise!

A coconut falls, they squeal with delight,
They dodge the fruit in the soft moonlight.
One thinks it's a UFO; he jumps in the air,
But it's just a coconut, their laughter's laid bare.

The night wraps them tight like a warm, fuzzy sock,
As the breeze tells the tales of each wandering flock.
With jokes as their compass, they roam and they play,
In the starlit serenade, they find their way.

Currents of the Lunar Sea

The moon's a big cookie afloat in the sky,
While fish sing sweet songs, oh me, oh my!
Sandy toes wiggle, in waves they do sway,
As the tides tell stories of mischief and play.

A crab in a tuxedo conducts his grand show,
Bringing all sea creatures to dance toe to toe.
A dolphin does flips, with style and flair,
As a starfish just rests, with a nonchalant stare.

They invent silly games with shells and seaweed,
And challenge the waves to a race, oh indeed!
The fish wear their hats made of kelp and of foam,
In the currents of laughter, they find their home.

Each bubble released brings a giggle and cheer,
As seagulls drop roasted coconuts near.
A party of giggles, in waves they delight,
In the currents of the lunar sea, they take flight.

Comfort in the Hush of Twilight

As day whispers secrets into the soft night,
A gecko croaks jokes as he takes to flight.
In hammocks that sway, the crickets all cheer,
As starlight tickles the laughter they hear.

A toucan in glasses reads the news with a squawk,
While a sloth brings the popcorn, a real slowpoke.
With giggles and whispers, they share stories old,
In the comfort of twilight, joy never grows cold.

A butterfly ballet twirls in the breeze,
While an owl starts a band with the rustling trees.
Each leaf tells a joke, each shadow a grin,
As the night wraps its arms, and the fun will begin.

With coconuts served in a tropical style,
The laughter echoes, stretching for miles.
The hush holds their giggles, the stars start to gleam,
In the comfort of twilight, they all share a dream.

Reflections of Stardust Dreams

A comet with sunglasses zooms by with flair,
While marshmallows float in the soft summer air.
Giggles erupt from the corners of night,
As owls wear bowties and bats take to flight.

They dip in the laughter like fish in a stream,
Catching the sparkles of stardust dreams.
A party of pixels in colors so bright,
As jokes tumble through in the shimmering light.

Fireflies twinkle their secret Morse code,
While a wise old tortoise hums a fun ode.
The moon is a mirror of all that they hold,
In the reflections of laughter, their stories unfold.

Under the gaze of the heavens so wide,
They dance like confetti, with no place to hide.
With every burst of joy that ignites the night,
In the stardust dreams, all the world feels just right.

A Symphony of Serengeti Sounds

In the jungle, the rhinos dance,
Wearing grass skirts, taking a chance.
Lions chuckle at the silly sights,
As zebras hum their jolly rites.

Hippos play the drums in the mud,
While monkeys swing and give a thud.
Giraffes look down with awkward grace,
And a parrot sings with a funny face.

The night brings laughter, wild and free,
With animals joining in harmony.
Even the owl gives a hoot and a wink,
A comical choir that makes you think.

Beneath a sky sprinkled with laughs,
Creatures dance like it's time for baths.
In this symphony of starry delight,
The Serengeti brings giggles each night.

Rhythms of the Insular Evening

On the beach, the crabs form a band,
Shuffling sideways, the funniest hand.
Seagulls squawk a high-pitched tune,
While seaweed sways in the breeze of June.

A coconut drops with a comical thud,
As palm trees sway, losing their bud.
The sunset winks, a brilliant show,
And surfboards giggle as palm fronds blow.

Starfish lounge like they own the beach,
While hermit crabs practice their speech.
Turtles in shades move in style,
Inviting all to join their isle.

Every night, the moon's a joker,
Tickling waves, the ocean's broker.
With rhythms of laughter lighting the way,
Insular evenings are here to stay.

Moonbeams on the Cocoa Shores

Coconuts wear a silly hat,
As crabs in tuxedos dance all flat.
The waves giggle, tickle the sand,
And fish in bowties make a band.

In the moon's glow, the dolphins leap,
Cheerful giggles, secrets to keep.
The cocoa trees sway with flair,
Rhythmic laughter fills the air.

A parrot performs a stand-up show,
Telling fish jokes with a flamboyant flow.
Nearby, a turtle takes a bow,
As the stars wink and say, "Wow!"

In this magic where laughter blooms,
Every wave brings amusing tunes.
Moonlit shores where joy's a chore,
Let's dance and laugh forevermore!

The Heartbeat of the Island Night

Bathed in laughter, the island breathes,
Whispers of fun sway with the leaves.
Fireflies twinkle, a playful fight,
As crickets chirp their heart's delight.

A mongoose jives in its tiny shoes,
Every step a punchline, what a muse!
Nearby, a frog croaks out a cheer,
As the stars nod, "We want to hear!"

Turtles slow-dance, a sight to see,
While the moon giggles, "Come dance with me!"
The ocean hums a merry song,
Inviting all to sing along.

In this heartbeat, joy flows free,
It's a festival of fun, just you and me.
So twirl and laugh through the gentle night,
Under the glow of mischievous light.

Beneath a Blanket of Beacon Lights

The fireflies flicker, dancing in my drink,
A party at night, why do I even think?
My nachos keep running, they think it's a race,
While I try to catch them, I'm losing my face.

With coconut bra on, I dance like a fool,
The crabs in the sand seem to think it's cool.
A parrot just laughed, dropped my drink with a splash,
As I wobbled and tumbled, I made quite a crash.

Laughter erupts from the shadows I see,
A troupe of wild monkeys, they think I'm a tree!
I join in their antics, and soon I am stuck,
All tangled and laughing—oh, what strange luck!

The stars up above shimmer, plotting some fun,
As I wrestle with sand, I'm losing, I've spun.
The night ends with giggles, the waves start to snore,
And I dream of my nachos—who could ask for more?

The Pathway of the Hidden Moons

The moonlight's a prankster, hiding in trees,
I trip on my laughter while dodging the bees.
A sock puppet contest, who knew it was here?
I'm laughing so hard, I can't even clear.

Sneaking a sip from a coconut jug,
I spot a lost slipper—oh, what a bug!
With stars as my witnesses, I dance with glee,
My foot in a flip-flop is now stuck in a tree.

A dream-giving dolphin swims by with a wink,
As I struggle to paddle, I start to rethink.
The tide's just a current, but I'm in a whirl,
Oh, night of the moon—let's give it a twirl!

With laughter in waves and giggles in sound,
I'll surf on a seahorse, my new friend I've found.
The night hugs my wildness, I'm ready for fun,
Tomorrow's adventures have only begun!

Star-kissed Fragrance of the Tropics

I smell something funny—perhaps it's my feet?
The ocean's perfume can't compete with this treat.
A banana peel slips, and off goes my hat,
With dolphins erupting, oh, fancy that!

The beach is a stage, well-lit and bizarre,
With seagulls applauding from high on a bar.
I step on a crab, and he clicks me in cheer,
Together we shuffle, oh, how we endear!

A salsa of salsa is brewing right here,
I'm dancing with pineapples, I have no fear.
The rhythm is wild, the stars start to play,
While the moon chuckles softly, enjoying the sway.

As laughter spills over, the night wears a grin,
The aroma of coconuts whispers within.
So grab me a drink, let's toast to the night,
For every giggle brings joy, oh, what delight!

Mysteries Unfolding in the Night

What's that? A shadow! Oh wait, it's my cat,
He's plotting more chaos, the mischievous brat!
With fins on his paws, he's ready to sneak,
But mystery's awkward—the neighbors all peek.

The stars are my witnesses, guiding me through,
I'm chasing a lawn flamingo, oh who knew?
He dances in circles—am I losing my mind?
As the waves play a tune and the crickets unwind.

Ghost crabs are laughing, they're dressed up all odd,
A costume parade—I must give them a nod.
The seaweed is tickling my toes with a tease,
And the whispers of fish have me begging, "Please!"

As laughter abounds, I dive into fun,
With lanterns in hand, I'm the party's own sun.
The night is a riddle, and I'm quite the sleuth,
As mysteries unfold, I just follow the truth!

Twilight's Embrace in Paradise

As the sun dips low, crabs start to prance,
In their tiny dance, they think they can dance.
But they trip on their claws, and oh what a sight,
Who knew these sea creatures would dance through the night?

Palm trees are swaying to a tune of their own,
While monkeys throw coconuts, oh how they've grown!
With mischief in air, and laughter at play,
Each moment's a treasure, come join in the fray!

Glowworms are twinkling, lights like a show,
While a parrot sings songs, though it doesn't quite flow.
But who cares for pitch when the beats are so wild,
In this paradise realm, we're all just a child!

As night wraps around like a warm, cozy shawl,
The stars peek down, it's a magical ball.
With giggles and whispers, we dance by the bay,
Life's a big party, so come out and play!

Echoes of Love Beneath the Canopy

In the jungle so lush, where the toucans swoon,
A goat and a llama both hum a sweet tune.
They argue about who can sing better, you see,
But the ocelot yawns, says, "Oh, let it be!"

Monkeys swing by, creating quite a fuss,
While the sloths take it easy, no need to rush.
A parrot joins in, painting chaos with cheer,
Who knew love could bloom when the lyrics are sheer?

The rhythm of night, with crickets on beat,
And the fireflies flash, making love feel complete.
An iguana just giggles amid all the fun,
As love notes in whispers float out one by one!

Underneath this grand canopy, hearts intertwine,
With laughter and grins, oh, how they do shine!
So dance with your partner, give twirls a big spin,
In this wild, wacky love, where all creatures grin!

Lullabies from the Coral Reef

Beneath the waves, where fishes gleam bright,
A turtle hums softly, a serene lullaby sight.
But the clownfish complain, "It's just not our jam!"
Yet they wiggle and giggle, it's all part of the plan!

An octopus twirls in a rhythmic embrace,
With eight arms a-dancing, just keeping the pace.
While the seahorses prance in a comical race,
Who knew underwater could feel like a space?

Starfish look on, with their unblinking stare,
As dolphins dive down, flipping high in the air.
With splashes and giggles, they make quite the scene,
Translating the laughter from sea floor to sheen!

In this ocean's giggle, where laughter runs free,
With bubbles and gurgles, we drift endlessly.
So close your eyes tight, let the waves work their charms,

In lullabies from reefs, we find warmth in their arms!

The Milky Way's Dance Over the Lagoon

As the moon starts to glow, frogs croak in delight,
With a tap of their feet, they jump into the night.
The stars wink at them, sharing secrets galore,
While a fish flips and flops, calling for more!

Here comes a raccoon, wearing shades like a pro,
He's sipping on coconut, putting on a show.
With a wink and a grin, he joins in the play,
Who knew the night sky would brighten this way?

The lagoon reflects all the shimmer and glow,
While the turtles compete in a splashy slow-show.
But with every big dive, the crowd just roars loud,
In the dance of the stars, it's a jubilant crowd!

So kick up your heels, and embrace the sweet sway,
As the cosmos above joins our giggles and play.
In this wild celebration, let worries take flight,
We'll dance 'neath the heavens, the joy feels just right!

Petals of Nightfall's Embrace

When the moon spills its silly beams,
The lizards dance to our crazy dreams.
Coconuts laugh with a clinking sound,
While palm trees play hide-and-seek all around.

A stray dog howls at a banana peel,
And every mango feels like a big deal.
Turtles stare at the stars with delight,
As crickets hop in a quirky fight.

The breeze sends whispers of ticklish air,
While fireflies giggle without a care.
We'll juggle with coconuts, oh what a show!
Who knew that night could be such a glow?

So let's toast to the moon and the funny glee,
With laughter and joy, just you and me.
Each wave that crashes holds secrets untold,
In this merry night, let the laughter unfold.

Celestial Haven of Kindred Spirits

In a hammock tied between two tall trees,
We sip fruit punch while swaying with ease.
Beside us the parrots squawk in delight,
Sharing jokes with the stars, oh what a sight!

A crab in a bow tie struts with great pride,
While the fish throw a party they can't quite hide.
The tide rolls in, with a splash and a cheer,
And seaweed dances, it's that time of year!

Underneath the blush of a pinkish sky,
We tell tales that make even dolphins sigh.
With laughter so bright, we forget all our woes,
What a grand cosmic meeting, anything goes!

Let's toast to the laughter and bonds that we weave,
In this wondrous night, we'll never leave.
As the stars wink and the fireflies play,
We'll find joy in the silly things they say.

The Twilight Glow of Paradise

As dusk stirs up all its shades of blue,
The toucans gather for a comedy queue.
With each squeaky giggle, the world seems to light,
Spinning tales of mischief in the soft twilight.

Two iguanas boast of their silly feats,
While frogs create music with tap-dancing beats.
Sandcastles wobble in fits of pure glee,
Waves stealing laughter like kids on a spree.

Swaying palms whisper secrets of fun,
With starlight twinkling, the night's just begun.
Let's leap like the dolphins or twirl like the breeze,
In this joyful chaos, we do as we please!

So grab a pineapple, raise it up high,
As the humor unfurls beneath the night sky.
Here's to the laughter, the joy that it brings,
In the glow of twilight, let our spirit take wings.

Where the Sky Meets the Ocean

At sunset's edge, where colors collide,
The waves giggle softly, no need to hide.
Jumping sea horses compete for the prize,
While jellyfish float with curious eyes.

A seagull named Gary, with a flair for the silly,
Drops sandwiches in search of a chili.
The laughter builds up like the tide in a race,
As starfish and shells join in the chase.

Sea cucumbers snicker, oh what a sight,
As crabs play charades in the soft moonlight.
Every splash is a smile, every ripple a cheer,
Where the sky embraces the ocean, we're here!

So gather your friends, let's share in the spree,
As the stars leap out for a brief jubilee.
With each grain of sand, let the laughter soar,
In the meeting of worlds, we can't help but roar!

www.ingramcontent.com/pod-product-compliance
Lightning Source LLC
Chambersburg PA
CBHW072128070526
44585CB00016B/1575